T0384658

Power UP

2

Home Booklet

Kathryn Escribano

With Caroline Nixon and Michael Tomlinson

1 A day on the farm

Where's Jack swimming?

Circle five more words → ↓. Which word completes the sentence?

m	o	u	n	t	a	i	n
t	o	r	t	r	o	c	k
o	l	l	e	a	v	e	s
c	l	a	n	c	e	a	a
p	x	k	o	t	o	n	m
a	d	e	s	o	r	t	e
n	f	t	g	r	a	s	s

Jack's swimming in the _____.

Window to the World

The Amazon water lily is from the Amazon River, in South America. Its leaves are very big. They're two metres wide!

two metres wide

What's two metres wide at home? Write.

At home, the _____ is two metres wide.

Tongue twister

Can you say this ten times?

Luke loves leaves.

2

Answer Jack

What's Daisy doing?

1

She's having breakfast.

2

_____
_____

3

_____
_____

4

_____
_____

Home mission

Make a book with seven pages. Ask someone at home to help.
On the cover of your book, write 'Me and my home'.
Keep your book.

1

2

3

Me and
my home

Days of the week puzzle

Write the missing days!

```
                              W
                              E
    ¹M  O  N  D  A  Y         D
           ²                  N
           ³                  E
                       ⁴S
    ⁵                         D
        ⁶                     A
                              Y
```

1 ___Monday___ , _____ and _____ have got six letters.

2 _____ and _____ start with the letter 'S'.

3 _____ , _____ and _____ have got the letter 't' in them.

4 _____ is my favourite day.

Window to the World

'Sunday' comes from the word 'sun', and 'Monday' comes from the word 'moon'.

In your language, which words do 'Monday' and 'Tuesday' come from?

the sun   the moon

Home rules

Write Daisy's home rules. Then write your home rules in your notebook.

> ~~get up early for school~~   have sweets for breakfast
> go to bed late   get dressed for school

I must ...

- clean my teeth after breakfast, lunch and dinner.
- _get up early for school_ .
- _____

I mustn't ...

- watch a film before I do my homework.
- _____
- _____

Tongue twister

Can you say this ten times?

She goes shopping and skating on Sundays.

Home mission

On the cover of your book, draw yourself with someone you live with, or stick a photo.
What do you do together? Write.

This is me and my sister, Ana.
We listen to music at the weekend.

3 Party time!

Guess who

- The pop star's singing.
- The cook's making a cake.
- The farmer's riding a horse.
- The clown's taking photos.

pop star   clown   ~~cook~~   farmer

1

cook

2

_____

3

_____

4

_____

Lost objects

Read and match.

The comic is for the tall man with short, straight black hair. The towel is for the tall woman with short, curly blonde hair. The CD is for the tall woman with long, curly blonde hair and the present is for the short man with a beard and a moustache.

Tongue twister

Can you say this ten times?

Peter Pirate's puppy's playing.

Why are you buying that?

Write Daisy and Jack's answers.

1

> Because I want to be a pirate.

_____
_____

2

_____
_____

3

_____
_____

_____
_____

4

Window to the World

In the world, the most common hair colour is black, then brown and then blonde.

What colour is your hair? Is it straight or curly? Draw, colour and write.

My hair is _____ and _____ .

Home mission

Ask two people at home, 'What's your favourite costume?' and write their answers. On page 1 of your book, draw a crazy costume using the answers. Write about the costume.

My dad's favourite costume is a pirate and my brother's favourite costume is a farmer. This is a pirate-farmer costume!

Jack's family photos

Read, look and write the numbers. They must add up to 17!

1. aunts
2.
3.
4. sons
5.
6. uncle's snakes
7.
8. cousins

1 Which aunt is shorter? _____2_____

2 Which son is older? _____

3 Which snake is longer? _____

4 Which cousin has got curlier hair? _____

____2____ + _____ + _____ + _____ = 17

Tongue twister

Can you say this ten times?

Frank's flat is on the first floor.

What's he saying?

theirs ~~mine~~ his hers

1. It's _mine_ .

2. It's _____ .

3. They're _____ .

4. It's _____ .

Window to the World

The Empire State Building in New York City has 102 floors and there are more than 1,500 steps on the stairs!

Count the steps on the stairs at home. How many are there?

The Empire State Building

Home mission

Draw someone from your family on page 2 of your book: an aunt, a cousin ... Show your picture to the people you live with. Can they guess who it is? Write about the person in the picture.

This is my aunt, Laura. She's got curly ... She lives in ...

9

Animal locomotion!

Write the animals' names in the circles!

| ~~atbs~~ | bbarits | roongkaas | lehwas | rrtoaps | philodsn |

They fly.

_____ bats _____

_____

They jump.

_____

_____

They swim.

_____

_____

Window to the World

Animals can be diurnal or nocturnal. Diurnal animals are awake in the daytime and they sleep at night. Nocturnal animals sleep in the daytime and they're awake at night. Penguins are diurnal, and bats are nocturnal.

Which other animals are nocturnal? Find two.

bats sleeping in the daytime

Wildlife park

Help Jack find the animals. Write.

pandas   bears   ?
?   ?   lions
?   kangaroos   ?

1 The ___lions___ are opposite the bears.

2 The lions are above the _____.

3 The kangaroos are below the _____.

4 The bears are near the _____.

Tongue twister

Can you say this ten times?

Can kangaroos climb?

Home mission

Ask someone at home, 'What's your favourite animal?'
Draw the animal on page 3 of your book, or stick a photo.
Write about the animal.

My mum loves pandas. They live in the mountains in China ...

Weather trail

Help Daisy get to the rainbow. Make a trail with seven more weather words.

IN →	🌧 →	💨 →	w	i	☀ →	s
	r	n	d	n	d	u
	a →	i	☁	o	l	n
	o	l ←	c	c	r ←	🌈
	u	o →	w	❄🌡	a →	i
	d	n	☀🌡	t	b	n
	❄ →	s	h	o	o	w → OUT

Window to the World

A rainbow happens when there's rain in one part of the sky and it's sunny in another part.
Learn the colours of the rainbow. Practise this sentence:

Ride **o**n **y**our **g**reen **b**ike **i**n **V**enice.

Match the coloured letters in the sentence to the names of the colours.

[r] red [ ] green [ ] violet [ ] indigo [ ] orange [ ] blue [ ] yellow

Crazy clothes!

Look at the pictures of Daisy's bedroom. Can you complete Jack's notes?

shorts   sweater   ~~T-shirt~~   coat   boots   scarf

Monday 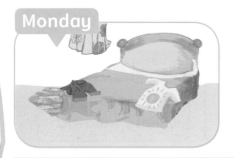 **Tuesday**  **Wednesday**

Monday
It was cold, but there was a ____T-shirt____ and _____ on the bed!

Tuesday
It was hot, but there was a _____ and a _____ on the chair!

Wednesday
There was snow, but the _____ and the _____ were behind the door!

Tongue twister

Can you say this ten times?

Walter wants windy weather.

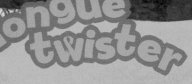

Home mission

Describe the weather today on page 4 of your book. Then ask someone at home, 'What are you wearing?' Draw the person and write.

Today it's cold and sunny.
My dad's wearing a green sweater ...

The best menu

Look at the menus and the food Jack and Daisy like and don't like. Choose the best menu for them.

Menu 1	Menu 2	Menu 3	Menu 4
vegetable soup meatballs	salad burger	vegetable soup pasta	salad cheese sandwich

	soup	burger	salad	meatballs	pasta	cheese
Jack	X	✓	✓	✓	✓	X
Daisy	✓	✓	X	X	✓	✓

- The best menu for Jack is number _____ .
- The best menu for Daisy is number _____ .

Tongue twister

Can you say this ten times?

Paula's putting the pasta on the plate.

14

Daisy or Jack?

What did Daisy and Jack do yesterday? Look, read and write *Daisy* or *Jack*.

1

I carried the plates.

Jack

2

I washed the cups.

_____

3

I cut the onion with my dad.

_____

4

I dropped a glass!

_____

Window to the World

Remember that to keep healthy, it's good to eat five portions of fruit and vegetables every day.

Which fruit and vegetables did you eat yesterday?

Look at the photo. Make your number 5 with fruit and vegetables!

Home mission

Ask three people at home, 'What has your favourite sandwich got in it?' and write their answers. On page 5 of your book, draw a 'super sandwich' with all the ingredients. Write about it!

This is our super sandwich. It's got cheese, chicken …

15

Words for a day trip

Write the missing letters. Make a new word with those letters. What is it?

1	2	3	4
s _t_ ation	funfa ___ r	___ ar par ___	mark ___ ___

The new word is t_____ .

Tongue twister

Can you say this ten times?

Ten tickets to town, please.

What did Jack do?

Look and answer.

1 Did Jack get a DVD from the library?
   No, he got a book.

2 Did Jack buy some cake in the café?
   _____

3 Did Jack give Daisy a hat?
   _____

Daisy's list

Look at Daisy's list. Where does she have to go? Tell her.

library   ~~bus station~~
supermarket   sports centre

Monday	buy the bus tickets for school with Mum
Tuesday	buy some food for the party with Dad
Wednesday	go to my swimming class
Thursday	get some books for the weekend

On Monday, <u>you have to go to the bus station</u> .

On Tuesday, _____

_____ .

On Wednesday, _____

_____ .

On Thursday, _____

_____ .

Window to the World

The British Library is one of the largest libraries in the world. It's got about 25 million books!

Which is the largest library in the world? Find out!

Do you usually go to a library? What's its name?

The British Library

Home mission

Ask three people at home, 'What's your favourite place in town?' and write their answers. Choose one of the places for page 6 of your book. Draw the place or stick a photo. Write about the place.

My grandma's favourite place in town is the sports centre. She goes …

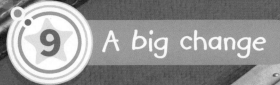

9 A big change

Look and write the words!

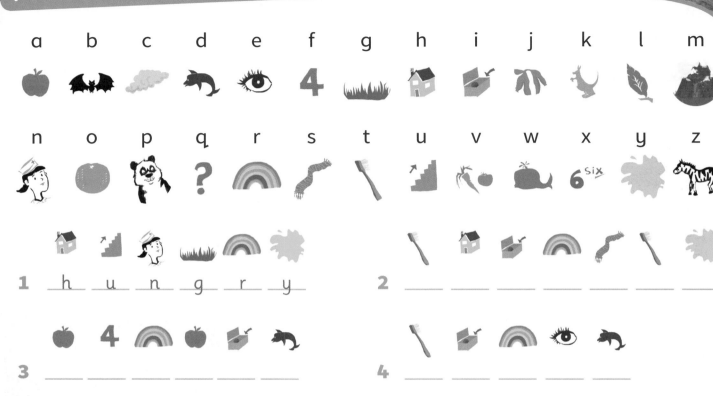

a	b	c	d	e	f	g	h	i	j	k	l	m

n	o	p	q	r	s	t	u	v	w	x	y	z

1 h u n g r y

2 _ _ _ _ _ _ _ _ _ _

3 _ _ _ _ _ _

4 _ _ _ _ _

Use the code to write more words. Show them to people at home.
Can they guess the words?

Window to the World

Wiley Post was an American aviator. He went around the world on a plane in 1933 – that's more than 80 years ago! He did this in seven days, 18 hours and 49 minutes. Now, you can fly around the world in 51 hours!

How many days are there in 51 hours? Find out!

18

What do you think? Look and write *A*, *B* or *C*.

  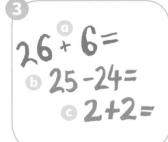 

1 ____ is more beautiful than ____ . ____ is the most beautiful.

2 ____ is more exciting than ____ . ____ is the most exciting.

3 ____ is more difficult than ____ . ____ is the most difficult.

4 ____ is more dangerous than ____ . ____ is the most dangerous.

Tongue twister

Can you say this ten times?

Here's Henry the hungry horse!

Home mission

Ask three people at home, 'What's the most exciting place to visit?' and write their answers. Choose one of the places for page 7 of your book. Draw the place or stick a photo. Write about the place. This is the last page of your book. Congratulations!

These are the Victoria Falls, in Africa. It's my dad's most exciting place to visit.

Countryside

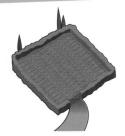
field

forest

grass

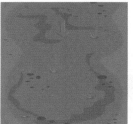
ground

lake

leaf / leaves

mountain

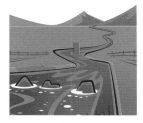
river

rock

tractor

Say the name of a forest, a mountain and a river from your country.

Daily routines

get dressed

get up

have a shower

have breakfast

toothbrush

toothpaste

towel

wake up

What time do you …? Choose three activities.

Days of the week

Monday

Tuesday

Wednesday

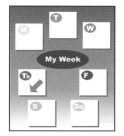
Thursday

Friday

Saturday

Sunday

 Which day comes after Tuesday and before Thursday?

Free time activities

go shopping

go skating

listen to a CD

listen to music

read a comic

watch a DVD

watch films

write an email

 What do you like doing? Say three things.

Jobs and parties

clown

cook

dentist

doctor

farmer

film star

nurse

pirate

pop star

present

treasure

  Which is your favourite costume?

Physical descriptions

beard

blonde

curly

fair

fat

moustache

short

straight

tall

thin

 Describe a person from your favourite TV show.

Extended family

aunt

cousin

daughter

granddaughter

grandparents

grandson

parents

son

uncle

Can you think of five more family words?

In and around the home

balcony

basement

downstairs

ground floor

first floor

second floor

inside

lift

outside

roof

stairs

upstairs

At school, which floor is your classroom on?

Wild and domestic animals

bat   bear   cage   dolphin   kangaroo   lion

panda   parrot   penguin   rabbit   whale

Can you think of five more animals?

Action verbs

climb   fall   fly   hide   jump

lose   move   run   walk

Choose five actions. How do you do them?

The weather

cloud

cold

hot

rain

rainbow

snow

sunny

wind

 **What's the weather like today?**

Clothes

boots

coat

put on

scarf

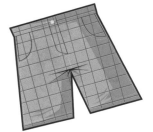
shorts

sweater

T-shirt

take off

 **What are you wearing today?**

Food

bottle   bowl   cheese   cup   glass   pasta

plate   salad   sandwich   soup   vegetables

What can you drink in a glass? What can you eat in a bowl?

Actions in the kitchen

boil   carry   cook   cry

cut   drop   fry   wash

Do you help in the kitchen? What do you do?

A day trip

 car park

 city centre

 funfair

 map

 ride

 road

 station

 ticket

 trip

What's the name of a funfair where you live?
What's your favourite ride?

Places in town

 bus station

 café

 cinema

 hospital

 library

 market

 shopping centre

 sports centre

 square

 supermarket

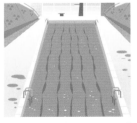 swimming pool

Choose three places. How often do you go to them?

Adjectives for opinions and feelings

afraid   boring   dangerous   difficult   easy   exciting

frightened   hungry   thirsty   tired   surprised

  Choose five adjectives. Act them out!

A new adventure

adventure   busy   email   round

text / send a text   travel   world

Close your eyes. How many adventure words can you remember?

My picture dictionary

Draw and write words you know in English.

My picture dictionary

Draw and write words you know in English.

My picture dictionary

Draw and write words you know in English.

My picture dictionary

Draw and write words you know in English.

31